Letters from the Devil to a Wife

Table of Contents

Introduction Exposing the Enemy's Playbook 5
Day 1 Rejecting God's Design 11
Day 2 Pride in Leadership 15
Day 3 Using God for Control 19
Day 4 Subtle Contempt 25
Day 5 Undermining in Public 29
Day 6 Words of Destruction 35
Day 7 Spirit Breaker 39
Day 8 Undermining His Work 43
Day 9 Greener Grass 49
Day 10 Moving Goalposts 53
Day 11 Craving Outside Desire 57
Day 12 Entitlement Over Appreciation 61
Day 13 A Home Without Heart 67
Day 14 Busyness as Barrier 71
Day 15 Technology as Barrier 75
Day 16 Persistent Negativity 79
Day 17 Suspicion as Default 85
Day 18 Selective History 89
Day 19 Assuming Incompetence 93
Day 20 Money and Control 97
Day 21 Denying Connection 103
Day 22 Intimacy as Control 107
Day 23 Unbalanced Expectations 111
Day 24 Children as Pawns 117

Day 25 Divided Loyalties 121
Day 26 Isolating Him 125
Day 27 The Path Forward 131
Day 28 Becoming a Builder 135
Day 29 Practicing Forgiveness 139
Day 30 Renewing Your Mind 143
Closing Words 147
Your Journey Continues Through Others 151

Introduction
Exposing the Enemy's Playbook

Make no mistake: there is a strategic assault taking place on the institution of marriage. It is not random. It is not accidental. It is a calculated campaign by the enemy to destroy what God has joined together.

The statistics tell a sobering story. Nearly 50% of marriages end in divorce. Countless others persist in silent disconnection—physically present but emotionally absent. Each dissolved union creates a domino effect that extends far beyond two individuals, affecting children, extended families, churches, and ultimately society itself. When marriages crumble, the foundation of our communities weakens.

Why does the enemy target marriage with such persistence? Because marriage is not merely a social arrangement but a divine covenant that reflects the relationship between Christ and His Church. A thriving, God-centered marriage stands as a living testimony to His faithfulness and design. When husband and wife function in biblical partnership, they create a fortress the enemy finds difficult to penetrate.

In your hands, you hold intelligence gathered from behind enemy lines. These thirty letters reveal the adversary's tactics with uncomfortable clarity. They expose the whispers that have infiltrated countless homes—perhaps even your own. These aren't fictional scenarios created for dramatic effect. They are the actual strategies being deployed against wives around the world every day.

Each letter unmasks a specific method the enemy uses to weaponize a wife's influence against her marriage. You'll recognize some tactics immediately—they may have already gained a foothold in your relationship. Others operate so subtly you might not have identified them until now. All have the same objective: to transform what God designed for building into tools for destruction.

Exposure, however, is only the beginning. Each letter is immediately countered with Scripture's authoritative truth—the divine antidote to deception. The reflection questions aren't merely theoretical; they're designed to illuminate the path forward with practical clarity. This 30-day journey offers us both revelation and restoration—showing us not only what's wrong but how we can make it right in our marriage.

By the final page, you'll possess more than marriage advice. You'll have spiritual discernment to identify the enemy's voice in its many disguises. You'll have biblical wisdom to counter every strategy with truth. Most importantly, you'll have renewed vision for your divine calling as a wife and practical tools to rebuild what the enemy has tried to destroy.

The enemy has been writing letters long enough. It's time for you to write a different story.

PART 1

GOD'S DESIGN FOR YOUR MARRIAGE

Day 1
Rejecting God's Design

My unwittingly accomplice,

Continue your subtle resistance to God's design for marriage. What works best for us is to treat the concept of submission as archaic and offensive—an outdated relic incompatible with your equality and the modern woman's independence. You should view your husband's leadership attempts as threats to your autonomy rather than invitations to partnership. When scripture mentions headship, put your foot down and immediately deflect with examples of men who have abused authority.

When it comes to marriage roles, I advise you to reject the "supposed beauty" of complementary differences. Don't worry! Your resistance need not be dramatic—small sighs, eye rolls, and dismissive remarks work wonderfully. This pattern will eventually exhaust him, leaving leadership vacant for *your* taking. After all, everything would work out so much better if *you* were in charge, wouldn't it?

Ephesians 5:22-23 "Wives, submit yourselves to your own husbands as you do to the Lord. For the husband is the head of the wife as Christ is the head of the church, his body, of which he is the Savior."

Let's Talk: God's design for marriage reflects the relationship between Christ and the church—a *loving leadership* that serves rather than dominates, and a respectful response that trusts rather than resists. When we reject this pattern, we miss the beautiful dance of mutual blessing God intended. Submission doesn't diminish a wife's value or voice but creates space for the husband to fulfill his God-given *responsibility*.

I used to struggle with this concept for years! After all, I was raised by a strong mother who taught me that I was never to depend on a man. Many years later, my marriage paid the price. I was in constant battle with my husband and deep-down resented God for choosing men to lead the household. So, my tired husband stepped back and allowed me to be the one in charge for a while. And the role was overwhelming. I felt as if I was the one who had to figure it all out, make the most important decisions, carry most of the burden, take over when things weren't working out, work extra hard to control everything and much more. I was exhausted! I remember praying and telling God that I longed to be protected and cared for. It was then that I realized that this had been God's plan all along! All I needed to do was step aside and trust *Him*.

True submission springs from choice, not coercion—a strong woman voluntarily yielding out of respect for God's design rather than weakness. When we fight against this order, we often create the power struggles we fear, whereas embracing God's design often leads to the very freedom and partnership we desire.

Questions:

1. How has cultural messaging shaped your view of submission in marriage?

2. In what situations do you find yourself most resistant to your husband's leadership? Why?

3. How might truly embracing God's design create more freedom rather than less in your marriage?

Let's Pray: Father, forgive my resistance to Your perfect design. Help me see submission not as weakness but as my strength—a willing choice that honors You. Where I've sought control from pride or fear, teach me to trust both You and the husband You've given me. May our marriage reflect Christ and His Church in beautiful harmony, each of us fulfilling the roles You ordained for our joy and Your glory. In Jesus' name, Amen.

Day 2

Pride in Leadership

My ambitious apprentice,

Your desire to dominate rather than collaborate serves our purposes beautifully! Continue believing your way is inherently superior—your preferences more refined, your decisions more logical, your methods more efficient.

Maintain that confident assumption that without your direction, your household would surely descend into chaos. Remember how effectively you've trained your husband to await your approval before proceeding with any decision?

Continue wielding your intelligence and competence as weapons rather than gifts. Interrupt his sentences to correct minor details and sigh dramatically when he suggests alternatives to your plans. The goal isn't to build a home together but to establish your supremacy within it—this will ensure your home remains divided against itself.

Proverbs 14:1 "The wise woman builds her house, but with her own hands the foolish one tears hers down."

Let's Talk: The distinction between building and tearing down often lies not in our competence but in our heart's posture. A wise woman may indeed be capable and organized, but she uses these strengths to construct rather than conquer. Building requires humility—recognizing that our way isn't the only way and that sometimes efficiency must yield to relationship. When pride drives our leadership, we may maintain control, but we lose connection with our loved ones. The foolishness mentioned isn't about intelligence but wisdom—knowing that a well-built home prioritizes *people* over *perfection*. Our hands can create spaces of grace where others flourish, or they can crush spirits through our criticism and control. True wisdom recognizes that leadership's highest purpose is serving others' growth rather than asserting our superiority over them.

Questions:

1. In what areas of your marriage have you prioritized control over connection?

2. How might your strengths become destructive when pride enters the equation?

3. How could you use your capabilities to build up rather than dominate?

Let's Pray: Heavenly Father, forgive my pride that has built walls instead of bridges in my marriage. Help me see where my desire for control has masked itself as competence. Teach me to use my strengths to nurture rather than dominate, to collaborate rather than command. When I'm tempted to correct, interrupt, or sigh in disapproval, soften my heart with humility. Show me how to build our home with wisdom rather than tear it down with perfectionism. May I honor my husband not just with my words but with my attitude, creating space for both of us to flourish in Your design. Transform my leadership into service and my criticism into encouragement. In Jesus' name, Amen.

Day 3
Using God for Control

My spiritually manipulative friend,

I'm delighted by how effectively you've weaponized your faith! Continue prefacing your opinions with "God told me" or "I've been praying about this," making disagreement with you equivalent to resisting God Himself.

Use selective scripture readings as ammunition rather than guidance, plucking verses from context to reinforce your position. When your husband questions your interpretation, imply his spiritual immaturity is the issue. Suggest that if he were closer to God, he would naturally agree with you.

During disagreements, adopt a martyred spiritual posture—sighing that you'll "just pray about it," implying your superior spiritual commitment. This approach is particularly effective because it appears righteous while serving self-interest—the perfect disguise for my spirit of pride. By draping control in spiritual language, you make accountability nearly impossible while maintaining an appearance of devotion.

Scripture: James 4:6 "But he gives us more grace. That is why Scripture says: 'God opposes the proud but shows favor to the humble.'"

Let's Talk: Spiritual manipulation represents one of the most subtle forms of pride—using God's name to advance our own agenda. The verse reminds us that God actively opposes pride, including pride disguised as spirituality. When we claim divine endorsement for our preferences, we risk crossing into dangerous territory—using God's name in vain. True spiritual maturity expresses itself through humility that listens, respects different perspectives, and remains open to correction.

Faith should unite a couple in mutual submission to God rather than become a tool for one to control the other. What appears as spiritual leadership can sometimes mask spiritual pride—a posture God explicitly opposes.

Questions:

1. Have you ever spiritualized your preferences to give them more weight in discussions?

2. How might claiming "God told me" shut down healthy communication in your marriage?

3. What would truly humble spiritual leadership look like in your relationship with your husband?

Let's Pray: Lord, forgive me for the times I've used Your name to serve my own agenda. Purify my heart when I'm tempted to claim divine authority for my preferences or spiritual language to win arguments. Give me the humility to acknowledge that my husband's spiritual insights are just as valid as mine, and that disagreement isn't always a sign of his spiritual immaturity.

May I use scripture to guide rather than ammunition to wound. Replace my spiritual pride with genuine humility that listens, respects, and remains open to correction. Let our faith unite us in mutual submission to You rather than become a tool for control. Teach me to lead spiritually through service rather than domination, reflecting Your heart rather than asserting my will. In Jesus' name, Amen.

PART 2

RESPECT AND PERCEPTION

Day 4
Subtle Contempt

My skilled pupil,

I applaud your mastery of contempt's subtleties! That slight eye roll, the dismissive sigh, the quick glance heavenward—these micro expressions communicate disdain while maintaining plausible deniability. "What? I didn't say anything!" Your tone conveys what words cannot—that underlying current of disappointment and disapproval.

Perfect your ability to make him feel foolish without explicit criticism. When he speaks in public, that quick glance to others communicating, "Can you believe this?" When he shares an idea, that momentary pause before responding that suggests you're evaluating whether his thought deserves acknowledgment.

These seemingly insignificant gestures accumulate, creating an atmosphere where he constantly feels judged and found wanting. The beauty of contempt lies in its invisibility to others while being painfully visible to its recipient.

Continue treating respect as conditional upon his performance rather than inherent to his position as your husband, and watch as his confidence erodes beneath this constant, invisible corrosion.

Scripture: Ephesians 5:33 "However, each one of you also must love his wife as he loves himself, and the wife must respect her husband."

Let's Talk: Respect isn't merely the absence of outright disrespect, but the presence of honor communicated through our smallest expressions. The scripture pairs a husband's love with a wife's respect—both unconditional responses rather than earned rewards.

Our facial expressions, tone, and body language often reveal our true heart more accurately than our words. Contempt functions as relationship acid, gradually dissolving the foundation of goodwill necessary for intimacy.

What makes contempt particularly dangerous is how easily we justify it internally while denying it externally. True respect begins with a heart attitude that values another regardless of their performance—seeing worth in their personhood rather than their productivity. When respect becomes performance-based, we create an environment where fear replaces freedom.

Questions:

1. What non-verbal ways might you be communicating contempt toward your husband?

2. How do you distinguish between respectful disagreement and disrespectful dismissal?

3. How could you respect your husband's position even when disagreeing with his perspective?

Let's Pray: Heavenly Father, forgive me for the silent ways I've communicated contempt toward my husband. Convict me of every action that has wounded his spirit. Help me recognize that respect isn't just about my words but flows from my heart through my smallest expressions. Teach me to honor him not because he's earned it, but because You've called me to it. Replace my critical spirit with genuine appreciation, my judgment with understanding, my subtle disdain with sincere respect. Guard my facial expressions, tone, and body language that they might build up rather than tear down. Show me how to disagree respectfully without dismissing his worth. May I create an environment where he feels valued rather than evaluated, affirmed rather than criticized. Let my respect be unconditional, reflecting *Your* heart rather than responding to his performance. In Jesus' name, Amen.

Day 5

Undermining in Public

My socially savvy accomplice,

Few tactics surpass public undermining for destroying a man's confidence! Continue those seemingly harmless jokes at his expense, presenting them as "just teasing."

Correct his stories in front of others—"Actually, it happened on Tuesday, not Wednesday." Complete his sentences when he pauses, subtly suggesting he's incapable of articulating thoughts clearly. Share embarrassing anecdotes that highlight his mistakes while presenting yourself as the patient, long-suffering wife.

Notice how others laugh while he forces a smile, internally shrinking.

The beauty of this approach? It appears good-natured while inflicting maximum damage to his standing.

Should he object later, express surprise at his "sensitivity" about your "harmless comments." This forces him into an impossible position—either absorb the disrespect silently or appear overly sensitive by objecting.

Meanwhile, others witness his repeated diminishment, unconsciously adjusting their perception of him. Remember, public undermining ensures he feels unsafe even among friends, gradually isolating him from potential support.

Ephesians 4:29 "Do not let any unwholesome talk come out of your mouths, but only what is helpful for building others up according to their needs, that it may benefit those who listen."

Let's Talk: As wives, our words possess immense power—creating either scaffolding that supports growth or hammers that break down our husband's confidence. The scripture provides a clear standard for our speech: does it build up according to needs and benefit listeners?

Public undermining fails this test completely, serving neither our husband's needs nor truly benefiting witnesses. What we present as humor often masks disrespect that wounds deeply precisely because it occurs in front of others.

Building up requires *intentionality*—choosing words that communicate genuine respect, especially when others are present. Our public treatment of our husbands not only affects how others see them but also how they come to see themselves. The highest compliment to a wife's character is a husband who stands taller because of her words rather than shrinks from them.

Questions:

1. How might your public comments about your husband affect how others perceive him and how he perceives himself?

2. In what social situations are you most tempted to correct, complete sentences, or share embarrassing stories?

3. How could you build up your husband "according to his needs" look like in social settings?

Let's Pray: Father, forgive me for the ways I've diminished my husband with my words in front of others. Convict my heart when I've masked disrespect as humor or correction as helpfulness. Help me see how my public comments shape not only how others view him but how he comes to view himself. Guard my tongue that I might speak only what builds up according to his needs. Replace my tendency to correct his stories, complete his sentences, or share embarrassing anecdotes with words that honor and uplift him.

Give me the wisdom to make him feel secure rather than exposed in social settings. May my public treatment of him cause him to stand taller, not shrink in shame. Let my words before others become scaffolding for his confidence rather than hammers that break it down. Create in me a heart that genuinely delights in honoring him, so that others might witness the beauty of your design for marriage. In Jesus' name, Amen.

A Pause for Kingdom Impact

I always like to make a pause in my book to ask that if God has been ministering to you through these revelations of the enemy's strategies against marriage, please consider becoming an instrument of protection in another woman's life.

Is there a wife, daughter, sister, or friend whom the Lord is placing on your heart right now? Perhaps someone whose marriage is under attack, who feels confused about her role as a wife, or who is struggling to discern the difference between God's voice and the enemy's lies? God may be calling you to be the very person who places this spiritual warfare manual into her hands.

Marriage is under relentless attack in our generation, and so many wives are fighting battles they don't even recognize as spiritual warfare. By sharing this book, you become a watchwoman on the wall, helping to expose the enemy's schemes against God's sacred covenant of marriage. If you feel the Lord's leading, you can bless another wife by scanning the QR code below.

Would you also prayerfully consider sharing your honest testimony through a review? Your experience could be the confirmation another struggling wife needs to recognize the spiritual battle for her marriage and equip herself with God's truth.

"Rescue the weak and the needy; deliver them from the hand of the wicked." - Psalm 82:4

Day 6
Words of Destruction

My verbally skilled agent,

Never underestimate your language's destructive potential!

Continue weaponizing your words—those cutting remarks about his inadequacies, comparisons to other men who "actually help their wives," remarks about his family's negative traits you see in him. Perfect the art of criticism disguised as "honest and constructive feedback" and "I'm just trying to help you."

When angry, go for maximum impact—target his deepest insecurities and greatest failures! Remind him of past mistakes during current disagreements.

Use "always" and "never" generously: "You always forget important things," "You never consider my feelings." These absolutes create a narrative of permanent inadequacy.

During arguments, veer beyond the issue at hand to character assassination: "This is exactly why nobody respects you."

Master the false apology: "I'm sorry you feel that way" or "I'm sorry, but you provoked me." Remember, a wife's destructive words work like slow-release poison—continuing to work long after the initial conversation, as he mentally replays your statements during quiet moments.

Proverbs 14:1 "The wise woman builds her house, but with her own hands the foolish one tears hers down."

Let's Talk: Our words literally construct or deconstruct our homes—not the physical structure but the emotional environment where relationships either thrive or wither. The scripture presents a powerful image of a woman tearing down her own house "with her own hands"—suggesting the personal, direct nature of destruction through speech.

Words that tear down focus on character rather than behavior, employ absolutes that allow no room for change, and attack vulnerabilities rather than addressing issues. Building with words requires restraint during conflict, speaking to problems rather than personhood, and remembering that criticism should serve growth rather than punishment.

The wise woman understands that her words become the atmosphere her family breathes—either life-giving or toxic. Wise speech considers long-term impact rather than immediate emotional release.

Questions:

1. What patterns of speech most commonly emerge when you're frustrated with your husband?

2. How might your words be tearing down what you ultimately want to build?

3. How could you address genuine concerns without resorting to destructive language?

Let's Pray: Lord, I confess how I've torn down my own home with cutting remarks, unfair comparisons, and attacks on my husband's character. I pray that You forgive me. Please heal the wounds my speech has inflicted on his heart. Help me replace "always" and "never" accusations with grace and specific truth.

When frustrated, guard my tongue from targeting his insecurities or past failures. Teach me to address issues without attacking his worth. May my words become building materials for our marriage rather than weapons of destruction. Transform my speech into a source of life, encouragement, and honest communication that serves growth rather than punishment. Let the atmosphere of our home be filled with words that build up rather than tear down, creating a place where both of us can flourish in Your love. In Jesus' name, Amen.

Day 7

Spirit Breaker

My enthusiasm crusher,

Your ability to deflate his passions serves our purposes magnificently!

Continue responding to his excitement with cautious pessimism—"Are you sure that's realistic?" When he shares dreams, immediately highlight potential obstacles rather than possibilities.

Perfect that subtle sigh that communicates, "Not this again."

When he succeeds in small ways, minimize achievements with phrases like "Well, that's a start, I guess." Should he pursue new interests, question whether he'll maintain his new commitment, referencing past abandoned projects.

Treat his passions as inconvenient disruptions to *your* plans rather than windows into his heart. If he persists despite your discouragement, withhold emotional support—participate minimally, check your phone during his events, and afterwards focus on what went wrong rather than what went right.

Your consistent message should be clear: his enthusiasm is foolish, his efforts likely to fail, and his passions less important than yours.

Eventually, he'll stop sharing his heart altogether—exactly our desired outcome.

Proverbs 12:25 "Anxiety weighs down the heart, but a kind word cheers it up."

Let's Talk: The scripture presents a profound contrast—anxiety that weighs down versus words that lift up. As wives, we possess unique power to either multiply our husband's anxieties or alleviate them through encouragement. Spirit-breaking occurs when we consistently respond to enthusiasm with caution, dreams with doubt, and efforts with criticism. Kind words aren't merely positive statements but expressions that demonstrate we truly see our husband's heart and value their aspirations.

Often, our discouraging responses stem from our own fears—of change, disappointment, or financial insecurity—rather than objective assessment. True kindness sometimes means supporting dreams we don't fully understand because we trust the dreamer. When we consistently discourage him, we don't protect him from failure but rather guarantee a different kind—the failure to try.

Questions:

1. How do you typically respond to your husband's excitement about new ideas or opportunities?

2. What fears might be driving your tendency to highlight obstacles rather than possibilities?

3. What dream or interest of your husband's could you intentionally encourage this week?

Let's Pray: Heavenly Father, please forgive me for the ways I've crushed my husband's spirit with my words and attitudes. I confess how I've met his enthusiasm with pessimism, his dreams with doubt, and his achievements with minimal acknowledgment. Help me recognize when my responses stem from my own fears rather than genuine concern. Teach me to be a lifter of his heart rather than one who weighs it down with anxiety. Give me grace to celebrate his passions even when I don't fully understand them, to support his ventures even when outcomes are uncertain, and to offer the gift of my full presence when he shares his heart. Transform my sighs of dismissal into words of encouragement, my criticism into kindness, my caution into courage to believe in his potential. May my responses to his dreams become windows that invite deeper connection rather than walls that shut down his spirit. In Jesus' name, Amen.

Day 8
Undermining His Work

My crafty saboteur,

Your simultaneous criticism of his career while depending on his income creates perfect cognitive dissonance!

Continue questioning his career choices, suggesting better paths he should have taken. Remind him of friends earning more or receiving greater recognition. Keep expressing frustration about financial limitations while simultaneously criticizing the hours his work requires. When he faces challenges, focus on how these affect you rather than supporting his professional growth.

Treat his work as an inconvenience to family life rather than his contribution to it. Should he consider advancement requiring temporary sacrifice, emphasize immediate difficulties rather than long-term benefits. And if his work satisfies him, subtly imply he prioritizes career over family. Conversely, if he limits work hours for family, question his ambition.

This approach ensures he feels inadequate regardless of his choices—exactly our goal. Meanwhile, express your own career frustrations extensively, expecting his complete emotional support while offering none in return.

Colossians 3:23-24 "Whatever you do, work at it with all your heart, as working for the Lord, not for human masters, since you know that you will receive an inheritance from the Lord as a reward. It is the Lord Christ you are serving."

Let's Talk: Work represents more than income generation—it's a primary avenue through which many men contribute to their families and fulfill their God-given purpose. The scripture dignifies all honest work as service to God Himself, worthy of wholehearted engagement.

When we consistently criticize our husband's work while benefiting from it, we place him in an impossible position—damned for providing too little, yet equally damned for the sacrifices required to provide more.

Supporting his work doesn't mean accepting negative patterns like workaholism but recognizing the inherent value in his contribution. True partnership means acknowledging the complementary nature of each person's work—whether compensated or not—and the sacrifices both make for family wellbeing. Respecting his work communicates respect for him as a provider, even while navigating genuine concerns about balance.

Questions:

1. How have you communicated value or disrespect for your husband's work?

2. In what ways might you be sending mixed messages about what you expect from him professionally?

3. How could you better support his sense of purpose and contribution through work?

Let's Pray: Lord, forgive me for the ways I've undermined my husband's work rather than honored it. Help me see his work as service to You and to our family, not merely a career or paycheck. Give me wisdom to support his professional growth without demanding impossible standards. Replace my comparison to others with gratitude for his unique contributions. Teach me to celebrate his successes and stand beside him in challenges. May I recognize that when I respect his work, I communicate respect for him. Let my words and attitudes create a sanctuary of encouragement rather than a space of criticism. Grant me perspective to see beyond immediate frustrations to appreciate his faithful provision. Thank You for a husband who serves our family through his labor. In Jesus' name, Amen.

PART 3
COMPARISON AND CONTENTMENT

Day 9
Greener Grass

My comparative critic,

Your habit of measuring your husband against other men creates magnificent dissatisfaction!

Continue noticing how your friend's husband brings her flowers "just because," while yours doesn't. Observe how thoroughly that colleague's spouse listens, unlike your distracted partner. Note the romantic weekend getaways other couples enjoy while your anniversary passed with minimal celebration. Maintain mental scorecards of others' thoughtful gestures while overlooking your husband's different expressions of love.

When scrolling social media, linger on those perfect family photos, assuming they represent everyday reality rather than carefully curated moments.

During couples' gatherings, watch attentively for interactions that highlight your husband's deficiencies. Should he notice your disappointment, deny making comparisons while continuing them internally.

Most importantly, focus exclusively on others' strengths against your husband's weaknesses—never a fair comparison of the total person. This selective perception guarantees perpetual disappointment—precisely our goal.

Philippians 4:11-12 "I am not saying this because I am in need, for I have learned to be content whatever the circumstances. I know what it is to be in need, and I know what it is to have plenty. I have learned the secret of being content in any and every situation, whether well fed or hungry, whether living in plenty or in want."

Let's Talk: Contentment represents a learned skill rather than a natural response—an intentional practice of recognizing value in what we *do* have rather than focusing on what we lack.

The comparison trap creates impossible standards by measuring our complete reality against others' partial, public presentations. When we consistently compare our husbands unfavorably to others, we create an environment where they can never measure up because the standard continuously shifts.

True contentment doesn't mean ignoring genuine issues but addressing them from a foundation of gratitude rather than dissatisfaction. Comparison steals joy by directing our attention toward perceived deficiencies rather than actual blessings. The "secret" Paul mentions involves recognition that circumstances don't determine contentment—our perspective does.

Questions:

1. How has comparison with other marriages created dissatisfaction in your relationship?

2. What strengths and expressions of love from your husband might you be overlooking?

3. What practice could help you develop greater contentment with your marriage's unique qualities?

Let's Pray: Heavenly Father, forgive me for the comparison trap I've fallen into, measuring my husband against others and finding him wanting. Open my eyes to see the unique ways he loves me that I've overlooked while envying what others seem to have.

Teach me the secret of contentment that Paul wrote about—finding joy in what is rather than longing for what isn't there. Help me to stop creating impossible standards based on carefully curated glimpses of other marriages. Guard my heart when scrolling through social media or gathering with other couples.

Replace my mental scorecards with genuine gratitude for my husband's strengths and expressions of love. Transform my perspective to see our marriage not as lacking but as uniquely blessed according to Your design. Plant in me a spirit of appreciation that nurtures rather than a spirit of comparison that withers. May I become a wife who celebrates rather than criticizes, who treasures rather than tallies. In Jesus' name, Amen.

Day 10
Moving Goalposts

My perpetually discontented charge,

I want you to work on your ability to move goalposts ensures your husband never experiences true success!

When he finally addresses one complaint, make sure to immediately shift focus to another unmet expectation. For example, after requesting more help with household tasks, criticize his methods when he complies. When seeking more quality time, find fault with the dumb activities he suggests. If he improves communication, complain about the specific words chosen.

You should master phrases like "Yes, but..." and "That's not what I meant..." to nullify his efforts. This approach is particularly effective because it creates the illusion that satisfaction is attainable while ensuring it remains perpetually out of reach!

Should he explicitly ask what would satisfy you, provide vague answers that preserve your right to disappointment. The cumulative effect is beautiful—eventually he'll recognize the impossibility of meeting your standards and stop trying altogether.

Even better, he'll internalize this failure as his own inadequacy rather than recognizing the game is rigged.

Proverbs 21:19 "Better to live in a desert than with a quarrelsome and nagging wife."

Let's Talk: This scripture uses striking imagery—comparing life with a contentious, never-satisfied wife to worse than existence in a barren desert. This powerful metaphor captures how constant criticism creates emotional desolation where relationship cannot flourish.

Moving goalposts transforms marriage into a performance evaluation rather than a partnership, with one person constantly adjusting standards while the other tries to meet ever-changing expectations.

True satisfaction isn't about perfection but *appreciation*—acknowledging genuine efforts even when imperfect.

When we consistently focus on what remains undone rather than what has been accomplished, we create an atmosphere of perpetual deficit. Healthy relationships require clear, consistent expectations and genuine recognition when those expectations are met. The opposite of a quarrelsome spirit isn't silence about legitimate concerns but addressing them with both truth and grace.

Questions:

1. How might you be moving goalposts in your relationship?

2. When your husband makes efforts to meet your requests, how do you typically respond?

3. How could you maintain healthy standards while still expressing genuine appreciation for his progress?

Let's Pray: Father, forgive me for the ways I've made my husband feel he can never measure up. I confess how I've moved goalposts, shifted expectations, and remained unsatisfied with his genuine efforts to please me. Help me recognize when I criticize his methods rather than appreciate his help. Open my eyes to see how my constant criticism creates a desert where our love cannot flourish and teach me to communicate clear expectations and to celebrate progress rather than demanding perfection. Replace any quarrelsome spirit with a heart of appreciation that acknowledges growth and effort. May I become a wife who brings refreshment rather than exhaustion, who offers grace alongside truth. Let my husband find in me, not an impossible standard, but a grateful partner who sees his heart and values his contributions. Transform my discontentment into appreciation for the man You've given me. In Jesus' name, Amen.

Day 11
Craving Outside Desire

My attention-seeking student,

Your hunger for external validation serves our purposes beautifully!

Continue subtly seeking male attention beyond your marriage—those seemingly innocent text exchanges with male colleagues, slightly longer-than-necessary conversations at social gatherings, and strategic outfit choices that draw attention.

Maintain those social media accounts that function as validation slot machines—each like and comment providing momentary satisfaction.

Cherish compliments from other men while dismissing similar words from your husband as merely obligatory. When he expresses concern about these patterns, label him "controlling" or "insecure" rather than considering the legitimacy of his feelings.

Justify your behavior as "just being friendly" while knowing the emotional gratification you receive. Remember, this approach works most effectively when kept in ambiguous territory—actions defensible individually while constituting a pattern of seeking emotional connection outside your marriage.

This divided attention guarantees your relationship never receives full investment—exactly our goal.

1 Timothy 2:9-10 "I also want the women to dress modestly, with decency and propriety, adorning themselves, not with elaborate hairstyles or gold or pearls or expensive clothes, but with good deeds, appropriate for women who profess to worship God."

Let's Talk: While this scripture specifically addresses physical appearance, the underlying principle speaks to *where* we seek validation and how we present ourselves to the world. True beauty and worth come from character rather than external validation or attention.

Seeking affirmation primarily outside marriage creates divided loyalty that is dangerous and diminishes intimacy with your husband. This doesn't suggest friendship with others is inappropriate, but rather that intentionally cultivating male admiration crosses important boundaries.

Modesty in this context isn't merely about clothing but about a heart that doesn't seek to draw attention away from God or appropriate relationships. When we consistently look outside our marriage for emotional fulfillment, we create vulnerabilities that can lead to greater compromise. Contentment with our husband's admiration rather than craving wider approval reflects secure attachment to both God and spouse.

Questions:

1. In what ways might you be seeking emotional fulfillment or validation outside your marriage?

2. How has technology or social media complicated boundaries in your relationships?

3. How could you direct your desire for connection more fully toward your husband?

Let's Pray: Lord, forgive me for seeking validation outside my marriage rather than finding it in Your love and my husband's devotion. I confess how I've craved attention from others—through choices meant to draw admiring eyes. Help me recognize when I dismiss my husband's concern as controlling while justifying my own behavior. May I find my worth in Your unchanging love rather than the fleeting approval of others.

Give me wisdom to establish healthy boundaries in my relationships, especially in this digital age. Redirect my desire for connection fully toward my husband, investing in our intimacy rather than seeking emotional fulfillment elsewhere. Transform my heart to value character over attention, modesty over admiration, and faithfulness over flattery. Let me adorn myself with good deeds and integrity rather than seeking to capture wandering eyes. In Jesus' name, Amen.

Day 12
Entitlement Over Appreciation

My entitled protégé,

Your focus on unmet expectations rather than received blessings creates perfect unhappiness!

Continue mentally cataloging everything your husband *doesn't* provide—experiences friends enjoy, material possessions others have acquired, romantic gestures you deserve. Treat his regular contributions as merely meeting minimum requirements while viewing special efforts as simply catching up to what should be standard.

When he provides financially, focus on budget limitations rather than his consistent work. When he helps around the house, note what remains undone rather than what he accomplished. Maintain an accounting ledger mentality—meticulously tracking *your* contributions while minimizing his.

During disagreements, quickly reference sacrifices you've made while dismissing his as expected. This approach ensures you interpret his actions through a lens of deficit rather than generosity. Remember, gratitude creates joy while entitlement guarantees disappointment—making the latter essential to our purposes.

1 Thessalonians 5:18 "Give thanks in all circumstances; for this is God's will for you in Christ Jesus."

Let's Talk: Gratitude represents a powerful spiritual practice that reorients our perspective from what's missing to what's present. The verse doesn't suggest thanking God for difficult circumstances but finding reasons for gratitude within them. Entitlement focuses on comparing what we have against what we believe we deserve, while appreciation recognizes the gift in what we've received regardless of expectations.

When we consistently emphasize what our husband doesn't provide rather than what he does, we create an atmosphere where his efforts feel futile rather than valued. Our mental accounting systems often overvalue *our* contributions while undervaluing others'—a natural but destructive bias. Choosing to deliberately notice and verbalize appreciation rewires our thinking toward contentment rather than comparison.

Questions:

1. What contributions from your husband might you be taking for granted?

2. How might focusing on what you "deserve" be creating resentment in your marriage?

3. What practice could help you develop greater appreciation for your husband's efforts and for what you have?

Let's Pray: Dear Lord, forgive me for the moments I've focused on what's missing rather than the blessings You've provided through my husband. Open my eyes to see his efforts, his sacrifices, and his love as the gifts they truly are. Replace my mental ledger of expectations with a heart of thanksgiving.

Help me to celebrate what he does rather than dwelling on what remains undone. Teach me to express gratitude freely and often, knowing that appreciation nourishes our connection while entitlement erodes it.

Thank You for the unique ways he reveals Your provision in our marriage. May I cherish what we have instead of comparing it to what others possess. Transform my perspective until I see our relationship through Your eyes of grace. In Jesus' name, Amen.

PART 4

THE HEART OF THE HOME

Day 13
A Home Without Heart

My image-conscious apprentice,

Your prioritization of appearance over the atmosphere in your dwelling creates the perfect heartless home!

Continue focusing on maintaining magazine-worthy spaces rather than creating places of connection. Enforce rigid standards for household organization while becoming irritated when family members actually live in the space.

React to spills and messes with disproportionate distress, communicating that objects matter more than people. When your husband creates disorder through his hobbies or relaxation, communicate that his comfort threatens your standards rather than enhances your home.

Should guests compliment your beautiful house, secretly celebrate while ignoring your family's discomfort within it. Remember, a home that feels like a perfect museum serves our purposes far better than a slightly messy space filled with laughter.

Proverbs 24:3-4 "By wisdom a house is built, and through understanding it is established; through knowledge its rooms are filled with rare and beautiful treasures."

Let's Talk: The scripture presents a progression—wisdom builds, understanding establishes, and knowledge fills with treasures. Note that wisdom comes first, suggesting that true home-building begins with discernment about what matters most. While visual beauty and order contribute to wellbeing, they serve relationship rather than replace it.

A heart-centered home prioritizes emotional safety above physical perfection, creating space where family members feel valued regardless of their contribution to aesthetics. This doesn't diminish the importance of creating beauty and order but places them in proper relationship to the people we love.

The "rare and beautiful treasures" mentioned might include material possessions but certainly encompass memories, traditions, and connections that furnish our hearts rather than merely our rooms. Wisdom recognizes that physical spaces should serve human flourishing rather than human activity being subordinated to maintaining spaces.

Questions:

1. How might your concern for your home's appearance be creating tension rather than comfort?

2. What messages might your reaction to messes or disorder be sending to your family?

3. What adjustments could create better balance between aesthetic standards and emotional warmth?

Let's Pray: Dear Father, forgive me for the times I've valued perfection over people, when I've cherished order more than opportunities for connection. Help me remember that a home is measured not by its appearance but by the love that dwells within its walls.

Grant me wisdom to create spaces that welcome rather than intimidate, that invite rest rather than impose rigidity. When messes happen, give me perspective to see them as signs of life being lived, rather than standards being broken.

Thank You for entrusting me with making our house a haven. May my husband find comfort here, not criticism. May our home reflect Your values—where grace abounds, where forgiveness flows, and where each family member knows they matter more than any possession. In Jesus' name, Amen.

Day 14

Busyness as Barrier

My overcommitted subject,

Your strategic busyness creates the perfect relationship barrier!

Continue filling every calendar space with activities, creating a life where meaningful connection requires advance scheduling. Respond to your husband's spontaneous conversation attempts with distracted half-attention while completing "essential" tasks.

When he expresses desire for more time together, explain how your overwhelming responsibilities make that impossible—while continuing to add commitments. Train yourself to feel virtuous about exhaustion, wearing busyness as a badge of honor!

Should he suggest reducing activities, imply he doesn't value your contributions or understand their importance. During rare unscheduled moments, immediately fill them with productivity rather than presence.

Master the art of physical proximity without emotional availability—sharing space while remaining absorbed in individual activities. This approach ensures you maintain the appearance of shared life while avoiding meaningful connection.

Ecclesiastes 3:1 "There is a time for everything, and a season for every activity under the heavens."

Let's Talk: The wisdom of Ecclesiastes reminds us that life requires rhythm rather than constant acceleration. The scripture doesn't merely acknowledge different activities but implies their proper timing—suggesting that wisdom involves discernment about when to engage each aspect of life.

Busyness can function as an acceptable mask for avoidance, allowing us to appear committed to relationship while systematically preventing its depth. True intimacy requires margin—unscheduled time where genuine connection can occur without agenda or distraction.

When we consistently prioritize activities over our availability, we communicate what we truly value regardless of our words. Creating space for relationship doesn't happen accidentally in our culture—it requires intentional choices about what receives our time and attention. The question isn't whether our activities are worthwhile but whether they're worth the relationship cost they exact.

Questions:

1. How might busyness be functioning as a barrier to connection in your marriage?

2. What activities in your schedule could be reduced or eliminated to create more margin?

3. What boundaries could protect dedicated time for your relationship amid legitimate responsibilities?

Let's Pray: Dear Lord, forgive me for filling my days with endless activity while crowding out time for what truly matters. Help me recognize when busyness has become a barrier rather than a blessing in my marriage.

Grant me wisdom to discern which commitments deserve my time and which I can release. Teach me to create margin in my schedule for unplanned moments with my husband—space where conversation can unfold, connection can deepen, and love can flourish.

Thank You for the gift of my marriage. May I honor it by offering not just my proximity but my conscious and intentional presence. Remind me that being available to hear my husband's heart is more valuable than checking another task off my list. In Jesus' name, Amen.

Day 15
Technology as Barrier

My digitally distracted pupil,

Your device devotion creates perfect consistent disconnection!

Continue prioritizing screen interaction over face-to-face communication—checking notifications during conversations, scrolling through social media during shared activities, and maintaining constant digital availability to everyone except the person physically present. Perfect the art of physically sharing space while remaining mentally elsewhere.

When your husband speaks to you, offer the appearance of listening while continuing to engage with your device—those partial responses that demonstrate you've captured mere fragments of his words.

During meals, keep your phone visible for "emergency" checking. In bed, extend screen time to avoid meaningful conversation or intimacy. Should he express frustration about your digital distraction, defend your behavior as necessary connection to others or legitimate relaxation after a demanding day. This approach ensures you maintain constant partial attention—present enough to claim togetherness while sufficiently absent to prevent its depth.

Philippians 2:4 "Not looking to your own interests but each of you to the interests of the others."

Let's Talk: This scripture challenges our natural self-focus, calling us to actively attend to others' needs and interests. In our digital age, attention represents one of our most valuable gifts—and where we direct it reflects our true priorities regardless of our stated values.

Technology itself isn't problematic, but its capacity to fragment our attention creates unique relationship challenges. Digital devices offer constant novel-like stimulation that can make the familiar rhythms of relationship seem less engaging by comparison.

When we consistently prioritize digital interaction over physical presence, we communicate that the person before us ranks lower than distant connections or entertainment. Creating technology boundaries isn't about rejecting modern tools but rather using them intentionally in service of our most important relationships.

Questions:

1. How might your technology use be creating emotional distance in your marriage?

2. In what specific situations do you find yourself most tempted to choose digital distraction over personal engagement?

3. What technology boundaries can you set in place to protect quality attention for your relationship?

Let's Pray: Dear Heavenly Father, forgive me for the moments when my screen has captured the attention that belongs to my husband. Help me recognize how my digital habits create distance in the very relationship You've called me to nurture.

Give me courage to set boundaries with my devices and wisdom to use technology as a tool rather than allowing it to become a barrier between us. Remind me that my husband's words deserve my full presence, not my partial attention.

Thank You for the gift of connection that happens when we truly see and hear each other. May I honor my husband by putting down my phone, looking into his eyes, and offering him the precious gift of my undivided heart. In Jesus' name, Amen.

Day 16
Persistent Negativity

My pessimistic partner,

Your consistent negativity creates the perfect toxic atmosphere in your home!

Continue finding problems in every situation, filtering your experiences through a lens of disappointment rather than appreciation. When good things occur, immediately identify what could go wrong next or how they fall short of ideal. Perfect the art of deflating others' enthusiasm with phrases like "Yes, but..." followed by potential problems they've overlooked.

In conversations, gravitate toward complaints, criticisms, and concerns rather than gratitude or possibilities. When your husband attempts optimism, subtly mock his "naivete" or remind him of past disappointments that justify your pessimism.

Maintain mental filters that magnify negative details while minimizing positive ones, ensuring your perception remains consistently skewed toward problems. Should anyone suggest your attitude affects family atmosphere, defensively cite your "realism" while rejecting their perspective. Remember, persistent negativity functions as relationship acid—slowly corroding connection while appearing merely observant.

Philippians 4:8 "Finally, brothers and sisters, whatever is true, whatever is noble, whatever is right, whatever is pure, whatever is lovely, whatever is admirable—if anything is excellent or praiseworthy—think about such things."

Let's Talk: The scripture doesn't advocate denial of difficulties but rather intentional focus on what remains good despite them. This verse suggests that what we consistently think about shapes who we become and the atmosphere we create around us.

Negativity often masquerades as wisdom or discernment while actually functioning as a perspective filter that distorts reality by magnifying problems while minimizing blessings. Our thought patterns create emotional climates that affect not only our experience but also everyone who shares our space.

Breaking negative thought cycles requires deliberate attention to different aspects of our experience—not manufacturing false positivity but noticing genuine good that exists alongside challenges. The quality of our thoughts directly influences the quality of our relationships, as mental patterns eventually manifest in words and actions that either build up or tear our loved ones down.

Questions:

1. How might your thought patterns be creating a negative atmosphere in your home?

2. What triggers tend to activate negative thinking cycles for you?

3. What practice could help you develop greater awareness of positive aspects of your life and relationship?

Let's Pray: Dear Lord, forgive me for the times my words have brought heaviness rather than hope to our home. I confess how easily I slip into seeing problems instead of possibilities, complaints instead of blessings.

Renew my mind according to Your Word. Help me filter my thoughts through what is true, noble, right, pure, lovely, and admirable. When negativity rises within me, grant me the wisdom to pause before speaking words that would wound rather than heal.

Thank You for the gift of a new perspective. May my husband find in me a partner whose words bring life rather than discouragement. Transform my critical thoughts into gratitude, my complaints into appreciation, and my pessimism into faith that You are working all things for our good. In Jesus' name, Amen.

PART 5
TRUST AND CONTROL

Day 17
Suspicion as Default

My suspicious spy,

Your default distrust creates perfect relational insecurity!

Continue questioning your husband's motives, activities, and communications. Check his phone when possible, monitor his social media interactions, and track his location through shared apps—all while presenting this surveillance as "just being interested" in his life.

If he works late, question the necessity rather than accepting his explanation. Interpret neutral behaviors through a lens of potential deception—"Why did you pause before answering?" or "You seem distracted; what aren't you telling me?"

Should he express frustration about your suspicion, frame it as a trust issue he created rather than a pattern you maintain. This approach guarantees he feels perpetually under investigation rather than presumed trustworthy. The beauty lies in its self-fulfilling nature—your suspicion creates the very distance that then justifies further suspicion, accelerating the cycle of disconnection.

1 Corinthians 13:7 "It always protects, always trusts, always hopes, always perseveres."

Let's Talk: Love's defining characteristics include a remarkable quality—it "always trusts." This doesn't suggest naive gullibility but a generous perspective that believes the best about another's character and intentions when evidence permits multiple interpretations. The scripture presents trust as an active choice rather than merely a response to perfect behavior.

When suspicion becomes our default, we create an environment where even innocent actions are viewed through a lens of potential deception. True intimacy requires vulnerability, which becomes impossible in an atmosphere of constant suspicion.

Trust doesn't mean blindness to genuine issues but rather choosing not to manufacture problems through hyper-vigilance or assumption. Sometimes our suspicion reveals more about our insecurities than our partner's trustworthiness. The opposite of suspicion isn't ignorance but rather the courageous choice to believe in another's goodness until clearly demonstrated otherwise.

Questions:

1. How might your past experiences be creating unjustified suspicion in your current relationship?

2. What would it look like to extend the benefit of the doubt more consistently to your husband?

3. In what situations do you find yourself most tempted toward suspicion rather than trust?

Let's Pray: Dear Father, forgive me for the moments I've chosen suspicion over trust, questioning motives rather than extending grace to my husband. Help me release the need to monitor, investigate, and doubt, which only creates distance between us.

Teach me the brave vulnerability of believing the best, of interpreting actions through a lens of love rather than fear. Heal any wounds from my past that make trust feel dangerous rather than freeing.

Thank You for showing us through Your Word that love always trusts, always hopes. May my husband find in me a safe harbor of confidence rather than a courtroom of constant questioning. Transform my suspicious thoughts into prayers, my doubts into faith, and my fear into the courage to trust both You and the man You've placed in my life. In Jesus' name, Amen.

Day 18
Selective History

My revisionist historian,

Your selective memory serves our purposes brilliantly! Continue maintaining detailed archives of your husband's failures while developing convenient amnesia regarding his faithfulness.

During arguments, reference grievances from years past as if they occurred yesterday, demonstrating how meticulously you've cataloged his shortcomings. When he mentions past kindnesses or consistent provision, dismiss these as expected minimums rather than acts deserving appreciation.

Develop that perfect dismissive phrase: "One good moment doesn't erase all the bad ones." Master the art of emotional bookkeeping—meticulously tracking his debts while quickly forgetting his deposits.

When he apologizes for mistakes, accept verbally while maintaining internal records for future reference. This approach ensures productive conversations degenerate into historical grievance sessions, preventing resolution of current issues. Most delightfully, this pattern guarantees your husband feels trapped by an unforgivable past rather than invited into a better future.

Ephesians 4:31-32 "Get rid of all bitterness, rage and anger, brawling and slander, along with every form of malice. Be kind and compassionate to one another, forgiving each other, just as in Christ God forgave you."

Let's Talk: This scripture presents forgiveness not as an optional virtue but as essential spiritual practice reflecting our experience of God's grace. Selective history functions as memory manipulation—creating a narrative where failings outweigh faithfulness regardless of actual patterns.

When we consistently resurrect past offenses during current disagreements, we demonstrate that our forgiveness was conditional rather than complete -as the one we receive from God. True forgiveness doesn't mean forgetting harmful events but choosing not to use them as weapons in future conflicts.

The emotional bookkeeping described transforms relationship into transaction—a detailed accounting system where grace becomes mathematically impossible because debts always outweigh deposits.

Getting rid of bitterness requires intentionally releasing our right to punish past offenses even when the feelings remain. Compassion means recognizing that the person before us represents more than the sum of their mistakes—just as we hope others see us.

Questions:

1. What past grievances do you find yourself repeatedly bringing into current conflicts?

2. How might selective memory be creating an unfair narrative about your husband's character?

3. How could you practice true forgiveness in your specific relationship situation?

Let's Pray: Dear Heavenly Father, forgive me for the ways I've kept detailed records of my husband's wrongs while overlooking his consistent efforts to become a better man. Help me release the ledger of past hurts that I've held onto so tightly, preventing true healing in our relationship.

Give me the strength to practice genuine forgiveness—not merely saying the words but truly releasing my right to punish past offenses, as You have forgiven me. Remind me that just as You choose not to define me by my failures, I am called to extend that same grace to my husband.

Thank You for the freedom that comes with forgiveness. May my husband experience our home as a place where mistakes aren't eternally archived but where your redemptive power transforms our shared history into a testimony of Your grace. In Jesus' name, Amen.

Day 19

Assuming Incompetence

My doubting supervisor,

Your assumption of his incompetence undermines so effectively!

Continue taking over tasks rather than allowing him to complete them his way. Remember how you refolded the laundry he had folded? Keep providing unsolicited instructions for basic activities. Check his work as if reviewing a child's homework. Correct him in front of others.

A man consistently treated as incompetent eventually stops participating—creating exactly the detachment we desire.

Train your eyes to see only his flaws, becoming blind to his virtues. Cultivate a sense of intellectual and emotional superiority that justifies your contempt. Remain oblivious to how your critical spirit slowly erodes his confidence and wounds his soul in ways that no one else can.

Proverbs 31:26 "She speaks with wisdom, and faithful instruction is on her tongue."

Let's Talk: Respect includes allowing others space to contribute in their own way rather than imposing our standards as the *only* acceptable approach. The Proverbs 31 woman speaks with wisdom and faithful instruction—not criticism or micromanagement.

When we consistently assume our husband's incompetence, we communicate fundamental disrespect that erodes confidence and participation. True partnership means valuing different approaches and abilities, recognizing that efficiency isn't always the highest value.

Our husband's dignity deserves protection through our words and actions, especially in front of others. The wisdom mentioned in this verse includes knowing when instruction becomes controlling and when it is helpful and respects another's capability and perspective.

Questions:

1. How has your need for control manifested as criticism or correction of your husband's approach to tasks?

2. In what ways might your "help" actually communicate disrespect for his capabilities?

3. What area could you intentionally step back from, allowing your husband to handle things his way without correction?

Let's Pray: Dear Lord, forgive me for the times I've corrected, criticized, and controlled instead of honoring my husband's unique ways of contributing to our home. Help me see his capabilities through eyes of respect rather than judgment.

Give me wisdom to recognize when my "help" actually communicates distrust. Teach me to speak words that build up rather than tear down, to appreciate his approach even when it differs from mine, and to celebrate his strengths instead of focusing on perceived weaknesses.

Thank You for creating us as different yet complementary partners. May my husband experience our relationship as a place where his contributions are valued, his abilities are trusted, and his confidence grows through my genuine respect and appreciation. In Jesus' name, Amen.

Day 20
Money and Control

My financial strategist,

Your use of money as a battleground creates perfect ongoing conflict! Continue using phrases like "my money" versus "your money" rather than "our money," emphasizing separation rather than partnership.

When he makes purchases you deem unnecessary, respond with disproportionate criticism while defending similar expenditures of your own. Maintain detailed mental records of financial grievances while overlooking his consistent provision.

During disagreements, quickly reference financial irritations unrelated to the current discussion. Fluctuate between excessive restriction and impulsive spending, creating monetary whiplash rather than consistent patterns.

When discussing financial goals, focus on how his habits obstruct progress while minimizing your own contributions to problems. For maximum impact, either completely abdicate financial responsibility, burdening him entirely, or control resources so tightly he feels like an allowance-receiving child rather than a partner. This approach ensures money discussions trigger immediate tension rather than collaborative problem-solving.

Hebrews 13:5 "Keep your lives free from the love of money and be content with what you have, because God has said, 'Never will I leave you; never will I forsake you.'"

Let's Talk: This scripture connects contentment with security—suggesting that money conflicts often reveal deeper fears and needs beyond fiscal concerns.

Financial disagreements typically represent competing values and priorities rather than simply mathematical problems. When money becomes a control mechanism in marriage, we transform a neutral tool into a relationship weapon. The verse reminds us that true security comes not from abundant resources but from God's faithful presence—a perspective that can transform how we view financial challenges.

While practical money management truly matters, our attitude toward resources often reveals our deepest beliefs about security, status, and self-worth. Creating artificial financial division within marriage ("my money" versus "yours") undermines the fundamental partnership marriage represents. Contentment doesn't mean abandoning goals but rather pursuing them from a foundation of gratitude rather than fear.

Questions:

1. How might money be functioning as a control issue in your marriage?

2. What financial fears or insecurities might be driving conflict in your relationship?

3. What steps could create more partnership and less division in your financial relationship?

Let's Pray: Dear Father, forgive me for times I've turned money into a weapon rather than viewing it as a shared resource in our marriage. Help me release the grip of control, the mental scorekeeping, and the divisive language of "mine" versus "his" when discussing our finances.

Grant us wisdom to approach money conversations with openness and mutual respect. Teach me to see my husband as a true partner in our financial journey, valuing his perspective even when it differs from my own.

Thank You for Your promise to never leave or forsake us. May this truth free us from financial fears that drive conflict. Replace our anxiety with contentment, our competition with collaboration, and our criticism with grace as we steward together what You have entrusted to us. In Jesus' name, Amen.

PART 6
PHYSICAL INTIMACY

Day 21
Denying Connection

My physical gatekeeper,

Your strategic withholding of affection creates perfect emotional famine! Continue treating physical intimacy as a low priority easily displaced by fatigue, frustration, or distraction.

Maintain physical distance that communicates unavailability—separate seating, minimal touch, and body language signaling disconnection. Reserve physical affection for public displays that maintain appearances while privately establishing barriers. When your husband initiates intimacy, frequently respond with reasons for postponement that never resolve into later availability.

Create impossible prerequisites for connection: perfect emotional conditions, complete absence of stress, or resolution of all relationship tensions.

Should he express frustration about your physical disconnection, frame his desire as merely physical while yours represents deeper emotional needs, creating a false hierarchy of intimacy. This approach slowly transforms your husband from hopeful initiation to resigned distance—exactly our desired outcome.

1 Corinthians 7:5 "Do not deprive each other except perhaps by mutual consent and for a time, so that you may devote yourselves to prayer. Then come together again so that Satan will not tempt you because of your lack of self-control."

Let's Talk: This scripture presents physical intimacy not as optional but as mutual responsibility within marriage—a gift given rather than a reward earned. While acknowledging legitimate reasons for temporary abstention, it emphasizes the importance of reconnection, and the physical vulnerability created by extended separation.

Physical intimacy represents more than merely physical expression but rather a unique form of communication that nurtures emotional connection.

When we consistently prioritize other activities and needs above physical connection, we communicate messages about value and desire regardless of our words. True intimacy requires vulnerability—the willingness to be fully known and accepted—which becomes increasingly difficult as physical distance creates emotional distance. Creating a healthy intimate relationship involves honest conversation about needs, obstacles, and expressions of love that honor both partners' experiences.

Questions:

1. What patterns might be creating physical distance in your marriage?

2. How has physical intimacy become disconnected from emotional intimacy in your relationship?

3. What step could you take to initiate greater physical connection with your husband?

Let's Pray: Dear God, forgive me for the ways I've created distance rather than connection in our marriage. Help me recognize how my patterns of withdrawal have wounded our relationship and denied us both the gift of intimacy You designed for marriage.

Give me courage to move toward my husband rather than away from him, to prioritize our physical connection even amid life's demands, and to see intimacy as a beautiful expression of our commitment rather than an obligation.

Thank You for creating marriage as a sacred space where we can know and be known completely. May our relationship reflect Your design for oneness—where physical connection nurtures emotional closeness, where vulnerability is met with tenderness, and where love is expressed through the language of touch. In Jesus' name, Amen.

Day 22
Intimacy as Control

My manipulative tactician,

Your weaponization of physical intimacy creates perfect relational power imbalance! Continue treating physical connection as currency in your relationship economy—a reward for desired behavior or withheld as punishment. Master the subtle cues that communicate potential availability contingent upon his performance.

When dissatisfied with recent interactions, withdraw physically while denying any connection between your displeasure and physical distance. Conversely, when requiring future accommodation, increase physical attention temporarily while maintaining internal transactional calculations.

During disagreements, weaponize both the offering and withholding of intimacy to gain advantage rather than express genuine connection. Treat his physical needs as weaknesses to exploit rather than legitimate desires to respect. This approach ensures intimacy serves control rather than connection—reducing what should be mutual vulnerability to mere behavioral leverage. Most importantly, remain unaware of how this manipulation distorts sacred connection into cold transaction within your marriage.

1 Corinthians 7:3-4 "The husband should fulfill his marital duty to his wife, and likewise the wife to her husband. The wife does not have authority over her own body but yields it to her husband. In the same way, the husband does not have authority over his own body but yields it to his wife."

Let's Talk: The scripture presents a radically mutual vision of physical intimacy—each partner yielding authority rather than maintaining control. This mutual yielding creates a relationship where intimacy becomes gift rather than weapon.

When physical connection becomes transactional, we transform sacred vulnerability into marketplace exchange, diminishing its power to nurture genuine intimacy in our marriage.

Using physical relationship as manipulation tool not only damages our spouse's trust but distorts our own capacity for authentic connection. True intimacy flourishes in atmospheres of generous giving rather than strategic calculation.

The passage challenges both withholding as punishment and demanding as right—pointing instead toward mutual submission where each considers the other's needs as legitimate and worthy of response. Physical intimacy designed as safe harbor from life's demands becomes another performance arena when weaponized for control.

Questions:

1. How might you be using physical intimacy as a tool for control rather than connection?

2. What fears or insecurities might be driving your need to maintain power in physical relationship?

3. What would mutual yielding rather than control look like in your intimate relationship?

Let's Pray: Dear Heavenly Father, forgive me for the times I've turned what You designed as a gift into a bargaining tool. Help me see how I've used physical intimacy as currency rather than as the beautiful expression of oneness You intended for our marriage.

Give me a heart that yields rather than controls, that gives freely rather than calculates strategically. Teach me to approach our intimate relationship with generosity instead of manipulation, with vulnerability instead of power.

Thank You for the sacred trust of marriage where we can experience true connection. Transform my perspective until I view our physical relationship not as a means to an end but as a precious bond that reflects Your design for mutual submission and genuine love. In Jesus' name, Amen.

Day 23
Unbalanced Expectations

My double-standard defender,

Your application of appearance standards creates perfect resentment! Continue holding your husband to rigorous expectations regarding health, weight, fitness, and appearance while exempting yourself from similar scrutiny.

When he gains weight, express concern about health implications—while justifying your own patterns through age, circumstances or genetics. Carefully monitor his self-care habits while defending your different choices. Maintain detailed mental inventories of his physical changes over time while expecting complete acceptance of yours.

When preparing for social events, critique his appearance while expecting affirmation of yours. Should he mention your inconsistency, label him shallow or uncaring rather than acknowledging his desire for mutual standards. This approach guarantees simmering resentment beneath a veneer of health concern—exactly our desired outcome.

1 Corinthians 6:19-20 "Do you not know that your bodies are temples of the Holy Spirit, who is in you, whom you have received from God? You are not your own; you were bought at a price. Therefore honor God with your bodies."

Let's Talk: This scripture presents physical stewardship as primarily about honoring God rather than pleasing others and even ourselves—a perspective that transforms how we approach health and appearance.

When applied consistently, this view leads not to shallow physical perfectionism but to genuine care for the body as sacred space. Double standards regarding physical expectations often reveal our deeper insecurities—demanding from others what we struggle to maintain ourselves.

True intimacy flourishes in atmospheres of mutual grace rather than unbalanced expectations, where each partner encourages health while accepting the inevitable imperfection. Physical attraction remains important in marriage, but genuine connection transcends unescapable changes that come with aging and life circumstances. At the end of the day, honoring our bodies includes reasonable self-care while rejecting cultural obsessions with appearance that diminish deeper qualities of character.

Questions:

1. Where might you be applying different standards to your husband's appearance than to your own?

2. How could conversations about health and appearance become more mutual and less directive?

3. How can you have balanced expectations regarding physical care look like in your relationship? And, how can you encourage and support each other in your health journey?

Let's Pray: Dear Lord, forgive me for the times I've held my husband to standards I've excused myself from meeting. Help me recognize when my expectations become unbalanced, when I demand what I'm unwilling to give, and when I justify my choices while criticizing his.

Give me a heart that values our bodies as Your temples—not through superficial perfectionism but through consistent, loving stewardship. Remind me that true beauty flows from a spirit that honors You rather than from physical appearance alone.

Thank You for creating us to change and grow throughout our lives together. May our relationship be marked by mutual encouragement, by grace that covers our imperfections, and by love that sees beyond the surface to the heart. In Jesus' name, Amen.

PART 7
FAMILY AND RELATIONSHIPS

Day 24

Children as Pawns

My family strategist,

Your undermining of his parental authority creates perfect destructive division! Continue contradicting his discipline decisions in front of the children, forcing him to either engage in parental conflict or surrender authority.

When disagreeing with his approach, discuss your objections with the children rather than privately with him. Perfect phrases like "I know Dad said no, but..." or "Don't tell Dad, but..." that position you as the permissive protector against his unreasonable restrictions.

When children express frustration with his boundaries, sympathize rather than support his position. Subtly communicate that you understand them better, reinforcing their emotional alignment with you against him.

During parenting disagreements, emphasize his family-of-origin dysfunctions while minimizing yours. This approach ensures children learn to circumvent his authority by appealing to yours— creating division rather than family. Most delightfully, these patterns persist long after childhood, potentially affecting their future relationships with others.

Ephesians 6:4 "Fathers, do not exasperate your children; instead, bring them up in the training and instruction of the Lord."

Let's Talk: While this verse specifically addresses fathers, the principle applies to both parents—creating unified rather than contradictory guidance. Children thrive in environments with clear, consistent boundaries established by parents working as partners rather than competitors. When we undermine our spouse's authority with our children, we create damaging division that forces children into impossible loyalty conflicts.

Parenting differences deserve discussion, but private conversation preserves dignity while united presentation provides security. Supporting our spouse's parental role doesn't require perfect agreement but rather commitment to resolving differences without creating divisions.

Children naturally attempt to navigate parental differences to their advantage—our responsibility includes refusing this manipulation while modeling healthy conflict resolution. What appears as "rescuing" children from the other parent's decisions often actually robs them of the security that comes from consistent structure.

Questions:

1. How might you be undermining your husband's parental authority with your children?

2. What patterns from your own childhood might be influencing your approach to parental unity?

3. What steps could you take to present a more united approach to parenting while still addressing legitimate concerns?

Let's Pray: Dear Father, forgive me for the times I've undermined my husband's authority with our children, creating division where You desire unity. Help me recognize when my words and actions place our children in the middle of adult disagreements.

Give me wisdom to address parenting differences privately rather than publicly, to support my husband's role even when our approaches differ, and to present a united front that provides our children with security rather than confusion.

Thank You for entrusting us with these precious lives. May our children witness in us a partnership that honors each other's strengths, resolves conflicts with respect, and demonstrates the beautiful harmony You designed for families. In Jesus' name, Amen.

Day 25
Divided Loyalties

My family mediator,

Your prioritization of parents over husband creates perfect divided loyalty! Continue treating your parents' opinions as authoritative while your husband's remain merely advisory.

During disagreements, quickly reference your parents' perspective as evidence supporting your position. Share marital difficulties with your parents while presenting yourself sympathetically, creating powerful allies against your husband.

Allow your parents significant influence in major decisions—home purchases, career choices, child-rearing approaches—while expecting your husband to adapt to their preferences. When he expresses frustration about this pattern, frame it as disrespect toward your family rather than legitimate boundary-setting.

During family gatherings, prioritize your parents' comfort and traditions over creating new ones with your husband. This approach ensures your marriage remains effectively a threesome or foursome rather than a partnership—exactly our desired outcome. Better yet, these patterns typically intensify rather than diminish over time.

Genesis 2:24 "That is why a man leaves his father and mother and is united to his wife, and they become one flesh."

Let's Talk: The scripture presents marriage as requiring a fundamental shift in primary loyalty—creating new family identity rather than merely extending existing ones. "Leaving" doesn't necessitate geographic distance or emotional disconnection but rather clear recognition of primary allegiance to spouse over parents.

While honoring parents remains important, marriage establishes boundaries that protect the unique intimacy of the husband-wife relationship. When we consistently prioritize parents' perspectives over our spouse's, we maintain childhood identity rather than embracing adult partnership.

Building healthy extended family relationships requires establishing clear expectations that respect both connection with parents and primary commitment to spouse. This balance proves particularly challenging during early marriage years and major life transitions when established patterns meet new priorities. True "leaving and cleaving" means giving our spouse exclusive access to certain decisions, struggles, and experiences—creating safe space for vulnerability impossible in divided loyalty.

Questions:

1. How might your relationship with your parents be creating divided loyalty in your marriage?

2. In what decisions or areas of life might you be giving your parents authority that belongs in your marriage?

3. What boundaries might need establishment or strengthening to protect your primary relationship?

Let's Pray: Dear Heavenly Father, forgive me for the times I've placed my parents' and other peoples' opinions, preferences, and traditions above the sacred bond You've established between my husband and me. Help me honor the biblical call to leave and cleave, recognizing my primary loyalty now belongs to the partnership You've ordained.

Give me wisdom to honor my parents without compromising my marriage, to seek my husband's counsel before turning to others, and to guard our relationship from outside influences that would divide rather than strengthen us.

Thank You for the gift of family—both the one I came from and the one we're building together. May our marriage reflect Your design for oneness, where we stand united as partners creating our own traditions, boundaries, and future together. In Jesus' name, Amen.

Day 26

Isolating Him

My relationship manager,

Your control of his friendships creates perfect isolation! Continue subtly discouraging connections with his friends through strategic complaints about time away, criticisms of their character, or excessive demands around his absences.

When he mentions potential social engagements, respond with sighs or thinly veiled disappointment that forces him to choose between your happiness and his relationships. After he spends time with friends, create subtle relationship penalties—coldness, excessive questioning, or comparisons between his enthusiasm with them versus with you.

Paint his desire for male friendship as either immature "hanging with the boys" or potential dangerous influence rather than necessary connection. Should he maintain friendships despite your efforts, insert yourself whenever possible—joining outings, calling or texting during his time away, or requiring detailed reports afterward. This approach ensures he gradually sacrifices external relationships for false marital peace—leaving him entirely dependent on your approval and connection.

Proverbs 27:17 "As iron sharpens iron, so one person sharpens another."

Let's Talk: This scripture presents friendship not as optional entertainment but essential development—relationships that shape character through mutual influence. While marriage represents a primary relationship, it functions healthiest within community rather than isolation.

When we systematically separate our spouse from supportive friendships, we create unhealthy dependence rather than interdependence. Often our discomfort with our husband's friendships reveals our insecurities rather than legitimate concerns—fears about comparison, influence, or divided loyalty.

Healthy marriages make space for both partners to maintain appropriate relationships that provide perspective, support, and accountability. The "sharpening" metaphor suggests that growth often involves friction—a process that may appear uncomfortable initially while producing positive results over time. Supporting our husband's connections acknowledges that even the healthiest marriage cannot meet every relationship need.

Questions:

1. How might you be explicitly or subtly discouraging your husband's friendships?

2. What fears or insecurities might be driving your desire to limit his relationships?

3. How could you actively support rather than restrict healthy friendships that benefit his growth?

Let's Pray: Dear Lord, forgive me for the times I've subtly discouraged my husband's friendships through my words, attitudes, or actions. Help me recognize when my insecurities have led me to isolate him rather than support the connections You've designed for his growth.

Give me a generous heart that celebrates rather than resents the relationships that sharpen him, that refresh his spirit, and that provide the unique companionship of trusted friends. Remind me that our marriage thrives when we both have healthy community, not when we depend solely on each other.

Thank You for the gift of Godly friendship in our lives. May I actively encourage my husband to cultivate meaningful relationships that strengthen him as a man, knowing that the support, accountability and perspective he receives ultimately enriches our marriage as well. In Jesus' name, Amen.

THE TURNING POINT

Day 27
The Path Forward

My discouraged subject,

As your persistent advisor, I must register my objection to your consideration of change!

Those destructive patterns we've cultivated represent intelligence rather than dysfunction—protective mechanisms rather than relationship poison. Any attempt to identify these patterns merely creates unnecessary guilt rather than productive awareness.

Remember: your husband's flaws justify your responses rather than inviting your growth. Focus exclusively on how he should change first rather than your own transformation.

Your marriage problems stem from incompatibility rather than mutual contribution—*his* deficiencies rather than shared patterns. Maintain certainty that transformation requires *his* initiative rather than yours.

Should you foolishly pursue change anyway, attempt it through willpower alone rather than seeking your God, His Word, and godly community support.

Most importantly, expect *immediate* perfection rather than gradual progress, and abandon efforts after inevitable failures! This approach guarantees continued destruction while appearing to seek improvement—my perfect recommendation!

2 Corinthians 5:17 "Therefore, if anyone is in Christ, the new creation has come: The old has gone, the new is here!"

Let's Talk: The scripture presents transformation not as behavioral modification but identity revolution—*becoming* someone new rather than merely adjusting habits. Recognizing destructive patterns represents the essential first step toward change, but awareness alone cannot create transformation. This is why the verse grounds change not in personal determination but relationship with Christ.

Change begins with honesty about patterns without collapsing under the weight of shame, recognizing that conviction leads to life while condemnation leads to despair. The journey from old to new rarely follows a straight line—typically involving progress, setbacks, and renewed commitment rather than instantaneous perfection. Be patient.

While marriage involves mutual growth, we remain responsible only for our own transformation rather than controlling our spouse's. The good news remains that even longstanding patterns can change through persistent application of God's Word, prayer, grace, and godly community support.

Questions:

1. Which destructive pattern identified in this book feels most relevant to your marriage?

2. What obstacles (pride, fear, resentment) might be preventing you from embracing change?

3. What spiritual or community resources could support your journey toward transformation?

Let's Pray: Dear Father, forgive me for the times I've blamed my husband rather than examining my own heart, focused on his flaws instead of my growth, and chosen familiar patterns over the difficult path of change. Help me embrace the truth that in Christ, I am a new creation with the capacity to leave destructive habits behind.

Give me courage to identify the patterns that have damaged our relationship, humility to seek Your transformation rather than relying on my own strength, and patience to celebrate progress rather than expecting perfection.

Thank You for Your promise that the old can give way to the new. May our marriage become a testimony to Your redeeming power as

I take responsibility for my part in our journey, trusting You to work in both our hearts as we walk the path of transformation together. In Jesus' name, Amen.

Day 28
Becoming a Builder

My construction adversary,

I must vehemently protest your shift from demolition to development! Reject the builder's mindset that focuses on creating rather than criticizing. Maintain the delusion that identifying problems demonstrates superiority rather than addressing them demonstrates wisdom.

I demand that you continue measuring your husband against *impossible* standards rather than celebrating his progress. You must resist the temptation to notice and verbalize specific qualities you appreciate, maintaining vague generalizations at best. How else are we going to destroy your marriage?!

When your makes efforts toward change, I want you to remain skeptical rather than supportive, treating growth as temporary anomaly rather than meaningful progress.

Above all, focus *exclusively* on external behaviors rather than heart qualities, maintaining superficial improvement without deeper connection.

Should you insist on this building nonsense anyway, attempt dramatic gestures rather than consistent small actions that actually transform relationships. This approach ensures any construction remains unstable—impressive perhaps in appearance but structurally unsound!

1 Peter 3:3-4 "Your beauty should not come from outward adornment, such as elaborate hairstyles and the wearing of gold jewelry or fine clothes. Rather, it should be that of your inner self, the unfading beauty of a gentle and quiet spirit, which is of great worth in God's sight."

Let's Talk: While addressing women's physical appearance, this verse establishes a profound principle—that lasting impact flows from internal character rather than external appearance.

Building requires attention to what lies beneath the surface—heart attitudes that shape words and actions rather than merely managing visible behaviors. The "gentle and quiet spirit" mentioned doesn't suggest personality type but rather soul posture—internal serenity that responds from confidence rather than reacts from insecurity.

Building marriage requires focusing on foundation elements: respect, gratitude, attentiveness, and grace rather than merely addressing symptomatic issues. While identifying problems comes naturally, cultivating a builder's eye means intentionally noticing positive qualities and growth potential.

The building of a marriage happens through consistent small choices rather than occasional grand gestures—daily deposits that gradually accumulate into relationship wealth. Building focuses not on what our husband should become but on who *we* are becoming.

Questions:

1. In what ways might you need to shift from critic to builder in your marriage?

2. What specific qualities in your husband could you more consistently notice and appreciate?

3. What "building materials" (words, actions, attitudes) could you begin using more intentionally?

Let's Pray: Dear God, forgive me for the times I've been quicker to criticize than to construct, more focused on flaws than foundations in my marriage. Help me exchange my demolition tools for a builder's mindset that seeks to strengthen rather than tear down.

Give me eyes to notice and a voice to celebrate the specific qualities that make my husband who he is. Teach me to respond to his efforts with encouragement rather than skepticism, to recognize progress rather than expecting perfection.

Thank You for showing us that true beauty comes from within—from a gentle and quiet spirit that builds with patience, grace, and consistency. May I become a wise builder who creates a marriage of substance through daily choices that honor You and strengthen our bond. In Jesus' name, Amen.

Day 29

Practicing Forgiveness

My grudge guardian,

Your consideration of forgiveness threatens everything we've built! I need you to continue viewing forgiveness as weakness rather than strength—defeat rather than freedom.

You need to maintain detailed records of offenses categorized by severity and frequency for convenient reference! I want you to confuse forgiveness with forgetting, creating impossible standards that justify your continued resentment.

When considering release, remember: complete emotional healing must precede forgiveness rather than following it. Demand perfect repentance from your husband before extending grace, ensuring the cycle remains locked!

Should you foolishly pursue forgiveness anyway, make it conditional—a probationary status easily revoked upon future disappointment.

During disagreements, quickly reference "forgiven" offenses, demonstrating their active role in your emotional accounting system. This approach ensures wounds remain open indefinitely while maintaining illusion of spiritual maturity through occasional verbal forgiveness without actual release.

Colossians 3:13 "Bear with each other and forgive one another if any of you has a grievance against someone. Forgive as the Lord forgave you."

Let's Talk: The scripture presents radical comparison—we forgive as we have been forgiven by God—completely, sacrificially, and without contingency.

Forgiveness represents neither approval of wrong nor denial of pain but rather conscious choice to release the right to punish. This release liberates both parties—the forgiven from shame's weight and the forgiver from bitterness's poison.

Genuine forgiveness doesn't eliminate consequences or bypass necessary conversations, but it creates space for healing that punishment cannot produce.

Forgiveness often requires process rather than moment—a journey of release that may need repeated choices before emotions align with decision. The phrase "bear with each other" acknowledges that living in close relationship inevitably creates grievances that require both tolerance and release. Forgiveness functions as soil in which relationship can grow rather than merely crisis intervention when damage occurs.

Questions:

1. What offenses or patterns might you be holding onto that require forgiveness?

2. How might unforgiveness be affecting your ability to experience intimacy in your marriage?

3. What step could you take toward genuine release of past hurts while maintaining appropriate boundaries?

Let's Pray: Dear Father, forgive me for the times I've held onto hurts as weapons rather than releasing them in obedience to Your Word. Help me understand that true forgiveness isn't weakness but strength—not defeat but the path to freedom for my own heart.

Give me the courage to forgive as *You* have forgiven me—*completely* and *without condition*. Remind me that forgiveness doesn't require forgetting or denying pain but choosing to release my right to punish, even when healing takes time.

Thank You for modeling perfect forgiveness through Christ. May our marriage become a testimony to Your redemptive power as I practice the ongoing choice to forgive, creating fertile soil where trust can be rebuilt and love can flourish anew. In Jesus' name, Amen.

Day 30

Renewing Your Mind

My thought defender,

This has now gone too far! Your consideration of mental renovation deeply concerns me.

Continue allowing negative thought patterns to run unchallenged rather than subjecting them to Truth's scrutiny. Maintain those destructive mental narratives about your husband, your marriage, and yourself—they've become comfortably familiar even if demonstrably false.

When your God's scriptural principles challenge your thinking, quickly dismiss them as unrealistic ideals rather than transformative truths. You *must* allow emotions to dictate your reality rather than bringing your feelings under Jesus' authority.

React immediately to circumstances rather than pausing to consider deeper perspectives! Most importantly, attempt change through occasional inspiration rather than intentional training—ensuring temporary motivation rather than lasting transformation!

Should you foolishly pursue this mind renewal anyway, attempt it through solitary effort rather than community support and accountability.

Romans 12:2 "Do not conform to the pattern of this world, but be transformed by the renewing of your mind. Then you will be able to test and approve what God's will is—his good, pleasing and perfect will."

Let's Talk: This scripture reveals the profound connection between thinking and becoming—transformed minds produce transformed lives.

Renewal begins with awareness of existing patterns, continues through intentional replacement with truth, and culminates in new perspectives that recognize God's will as good rather than burdensome. Our thoughts about our husband, our marriage, and ourselves create interpretive filters through which we experience reality—often distorting rather than clarifying our circumstances.

Mind renewal involves intentional training rather than passive experience—the deliberate practice of identifying destructive thoughts and replacing them with life-giving alternatives. This process requires both grace and persistence, acknowledging that thought patterns developed over years require time to redirect.

The "pattern of this world" often includes cynicism about marriage, self-focused expectations of fulfillment, and quick resort to criticism rather than appreciation—worldviews requiring conscious rejection rather than unconscious absorption.

Questions:

1. What negative thought patterns about your husband or marriage have become habitual for you?

2. How might scripture challenge these narratives with alternative perspectives?

3. What practical biblical thought-training practice could help redirect your thinking patterns?

Final Prayer: Dear Heavenly Father, forgive me for allowing negative thought patterns about my husband and our marriage to go unchallenged in my mind. Help me recognize when my thinking aligns with the world's cynicism rather than Your truth.

Transform me by the renewing of my mind through Your Word. Give me the discipline to capture destructive thoughts and replace them with perspectives that honor You and my husband. Teach me to pause before reacting, to filter my emotions through Your truth, and to see our relationship through eyes of faith rather than frustration.

Thank You for the promise that renewed thinking leads to renewed living. May my thoughts become a garden where love, respect, and gratitude flourish, creating a mind that recognizes Your will for our marriage as good, pleasing, and perfect. In Jesus' name, Amen.

Closing Words

My dear friend,

Your journey through these letters has revealed the enemy's playbook—tactics designed to erode our marriages from within. But take heart! The same God who exposes darkness provides light for your path forward.

Remember that transformation isn't about perfection but persistence. When you stumble—and you will—don't allow shame to convince you that change is impossible. The enemy loves nothing more than a discouraged wife who abandons hope after initial failures. Instead, view each setback as an opportunity to experience God's grace anew and recommit to His design.

Marriage represents more than mere happiness—it's a sacred covenant reflecting Christ's relationship with His Church. When we choose respect despite disagreement, when we offer grace instead of criticism, when we pursue intimacy rather than isolation, we're not just improving our relationship; we're participating in holy work that testifies to God's faithfulness.

The most powerful changes often begin invisibly—in transformed thoughts before changed actions, in heart attitudes before spoken words. Your husband may not immediately notice or respond to your initial efforts. Continue anyway. Keep interceding for him. Transformation that depends on immediate validation rarely persists through inevitable challenges.

As you move forward, guard against three common deceptions. First, the lie that your husband must change first—scripture calls us to obedience regardless of his response.

Second, the illusion that dramatic gestures matter more than daily choices—consistency transforms more deeply than occasional intensity.

Third, the falsehood that you can accomplish lasting change through willpower alone—a partnership with God provides the strength that we as humans cannot sustain on our own.

Your marriage deserves protection through intentional boundaries around influences that undermine its health. Evaluate your media consumption, friendships, and family relationships through this filter: do they strengthen or weaken your commitment to God's design for marriage?

Most importantly, remember that your identity rests in Christ rather than your role as wife. When marriage becomes your primary source of worth, disappointments crush rather than challenge. When Christ remains your foundation, relationship struggles become growth opportunities rather than identity threats.

The enemy believed these thirty days would simply reveal how hopelessly far you've fallen. Instead, let them become the turning point when you recognized his tactics and chose a different path—a journey toward becoming the wife God designed you to be!

Hebrews 10:23-24 "Let us hold unswervingly to the hope we profess, for he who promised is faithful. And let us consider how we may spur one another on toward love and good deeds."

Your Journey Continues Through Others

As you close these pages, I pray your heart is filled with newfound clarity about the spiritual battle for your marriage and confidence in the victory that Christ has already secured for you. But this journey doesn't end here—it multiplies through you.

You now carry powerful revelations that could be life-changing for other wives who are still walking in confusion, unaware that their marriage struggles have spiritual roots. The truths that have set you free are meant to flow through you to bring freedom to others.

Consider this your commission: to be a light-bearer in a generation of wives who desperately need to see clearly. Every marriage that is protected and transformed creates a powerful testimony to God's design and a fortress against the enemy's agenda.

Please consider giving a copy of this book to someone who desperately need it or even starting a women's study group with this book to build each other up in your marriages and God-given assignments. There is incredible power when wives come together in unity, supporting one another in spiritual warfare and encouraging each other to walk in their divine calling.

If you haven't had the chance to share your testimony through a review, please consider doing so now—your words could be the very confirmation another struggling wife needs to recognize God's hand in her circumstances.

Scan this QR code or find the book on Amazon.com:

Finally, be on the lookout for my upcoming book **"Life-Changing Prayers"**—a 40-day journey that will take you even deeper into spiritual warfare and victory.

Here's a small preview:

GET READY—YOUR VICTORY BEGINS NOW!

You must know and keep in mind that *everything* is spiritual. Yes, *everything*. In this prayer journey, we will get into some of the deepest spiritual realities seldom addressed from the pulpit, exposing demonic strategies and spiritual attacks that operate in the shadows of our everyday lives.

In the next 40 days, you will begin to uncover and understand the enemy's intelligence networks that may be working against your life—revealing the true source behind attacks you never understood or circumstances you never thought to connect to the spiritual realm. That persistent financial struggle, those recurring negative relationship patterns, the unexplained anxiety that surfaces at crucial moments, or the way certain opportunities always seem to slip through your fingers. These are not mere coincidences but calculated spiritual opposition that has gone unrecognized and therefore unopposed.

God never designed you to live defensively or just survive until heaven. Through Christ's sacrifice, *YOU* have been given authority to experience victorious, abundant living right now. Instead of hoping your problems will disappear, you'll learn to engage purposefully in prayer, using biblical principles to overcome obstacles and step into God's amazing purposes for your life.

Your heavenly Father has an abundant life waiting for you—one overflowing with purpose, victory, and divine generational blessings. These powerful spiritual insights and prayer strategies will help you to step boldly into your rightful inheritance and take back everything the enemy has tried to steal from your destiny.

You must know that your breakthrough starts with prayer and your victory begins now!

Together, we rise as daughters of the King, equipped with truth and empowered for victory.

Your sister in this journey,

Waleska

www.ingramcontent.com/pod-product-compliance
Lightning Source LLC
LaVergne TN
LVHW041845070526
838199LV00045BA/1440